WORDS OF WISDOM

HANS CHRISTIAN ANDERSEN

JOLLYJOY

100 Selected Quotes
by Hans Christian Andersen

Edition 2024

Published by

JOLLYJOY

G/F, 4771/23, Bharat Ram Road, Daryaganj, New Delhi-110002

E-mail: Contact@jollyjoybooks.com

ISBN: 9789363976290

Cover, Typesetting, and Book Design by JollyJoy
Printed & bound in India

ABOUT THE AUTHOR

Hans Christian Andersen (born April 2, 1805, Odense, near Copenhagen, Denmark—died August 4, 1875, Copenhagen) was a Danish master of the literary fairy tale whose stories achieved wide renown. He is also the author of plays, novels, poems, travel books, and several autobiographies. While many of those works are almost unknown outside Denmark, his fairy tales are among the most frequently translated works in all of literary history.

100 SELECTED QUOTES

"But a mermaid has no tears,
and therefore she suffers so much more."

"Where words fail,
music speaks."

"When the bird of the heart begins to sing,
too often will reason stop up her ears."

"Just living is not enough,"
said the butterfly,
"one must have sunshine,
freedom, and a little flower."

TO TRAVEL IS TO LIVE

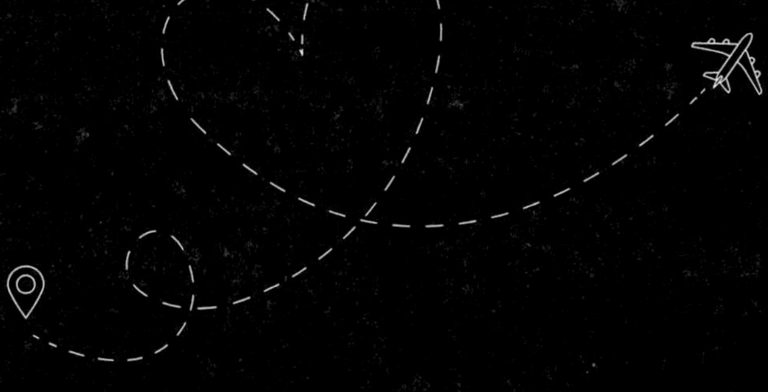

"To move, to breathe, to fly, to float,
To gain all while you give,
To roam the roads of lands remote,
To travel is to live."

"Enjoy life.
There's plenty of time to be dead."

"Life is like a beautiful melody,
only the lyrics are messed up."

*"Every man's life is a fairy tale,
written by God's fingers."*

"She laughed and danced with the thought of death in her heart."

"Life itself is the most wonderful fairy tale."

"The whole world is a series of miracles,
but we're so used to them we call them ordinary things."

"Everything you look at can become a fairy tale and you can get a story from everything you touch."

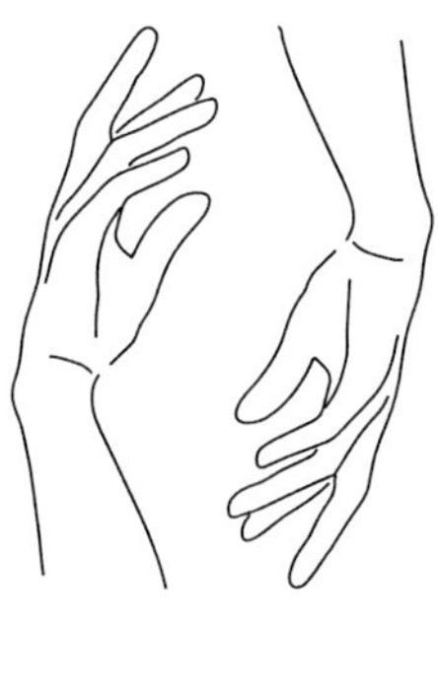

Human beings, on the contrary,
have a soul which lives forever,
lives after the body has been turned to dust.
It rises up through the clear,
pure air beyond the glittering stars.

"If you looked down to the bottom of my soul,you would understand fully the source of my longing and – pity me. Even the open, transparent lake has its unknown depths, which no divers know."

"To be of use to the world is the only way to be happy."

"Death walks faster than the wind and never returns what he has taken."

"You are a dreamer and that is your misfortune."

There was once a merchant who was so rich that he might have paved the whole street, and a little alley besides, with silver money. But he didn't do it – he knew better how to use his money than that.

"It doesn't matter if you're born in a duck yard,
so long as you are hatched from a swan's egg!"

MY
LIFE
WILL
BE
THE
BEST
ILLUSTRATION
OF
ALL
MY
WORK

"Never had she danced so beautifully;
the sharp knives cut her feet,
but she did not feel it, for the pain
in her heart was far greater."

"I know what you want.
It is very stupid of you,
but you shall have your way,
and it will bring you to sorrow,
my pretty princess."

"Brave soldier, never fear.
Even though your death is near."

"But shouldn't all of us on earth give the best we have to others and offer whatever is in our power?"

"His own image;
no longer a dark, gray bird,
ugly and disagreeable to look at,
but a graceful and beautiful swan.
To be born in a duck's nest, in a farmyard,
is of no consequence to a bird,
if it is hatched from a swan's egg."

I ONLY APPEAR TO BE DEAD

"Autumn came, and the leaves in the forest turned to orange and gold. Then, as winter approached, the wind caught them as they fell"

"Many, many steeples would have to be stacked one on top of another to reach from the bottom to the surface of the sea."

"Word is a shadow," said the shadow,
"and as such it must speak."

"He now felt glad at having suffered sorrow and trouble,
because it enabled him to enjoy so much better
all the pleasure and happiness around him;"

TRAVELLING

EXPANDS

THE

MIND

RARELY

"But he hasn't got anything on,
'A little child said."

"And they both sat there, grown up,
yet children at heart;
and it was summer, - warm,
beautiful summer."

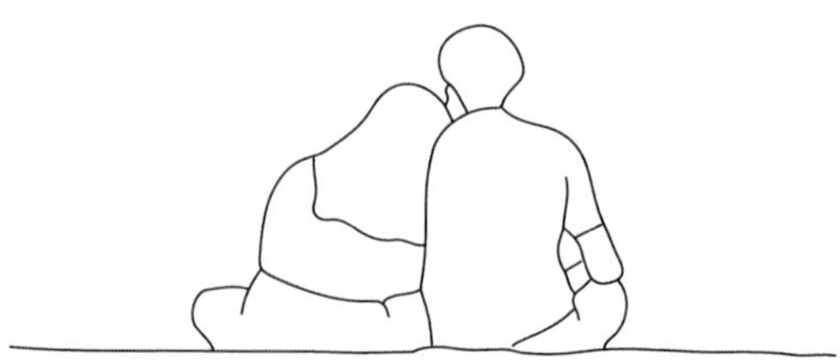

*"The wiser a man becomes,
the more he will read,
and those who are wisest read most."*

*"When we get to the end of the story,
you will know more than you do now..."*

"Every step you take will feel as if you were treading upon knife blades so sharp that blood must flow. I am willing to help you, but are you willing to suffer all this?" "Yes," the little mermaid said in a trembling voice, as she thought of the prince and of gaining a human soul."

"Almighty God, the only have I; thou steerest my fate, I must give myself up to thee! Give me a livelihood! Give me a bride! My blood wants love, as my heart does!"

*"I never dreamed of such happiness as this,
while I was an ugly duckling."*

"The good and the beautiful is not forgotten;
it lives in legend and in song."

I would give gladly all the hundreds of years that I have to live, to be a human being only for one day, and to have the hope of knowing the happiness of that glorious world above the stars.

*"It is only with the heart
that one can see clearly,
for the most essential things
are invisible to the eye."*

"Eighty percent of our criminals come from unsympathetic homes"

"This was the last evening that
she should breathe the same air
with him or gaze on the starry sky
and the deep sea. An eternal night,
without a thought or a dream, awaited her."

THEY MADE THEMSELVES COMFORTABLE

"In the days of Moses and the prophets such a man would have been counted among the wise men of the land; in the Middle Ages he would have been burned at the stake."

*"The sea is softer than your delicate hands,
and yet it can alter the shape of hard stones."*

"Farewell, farewell," said the swallow, with a heavy heart, as he left the warm countries, to fly back into Denmark. There he had a nest over the window of a house in which dwelt the writer of fairy tales. The swallow sang "Tweet, tweet," and from his song came the whole story."

"Some are created for beauty, and some for use; and there are some which one can do without altogether."

*"You may have thousands of my days,
but I have thousands of moments in
which I can be merry and happy.
Does all the beauty of the
world cease when you die"*

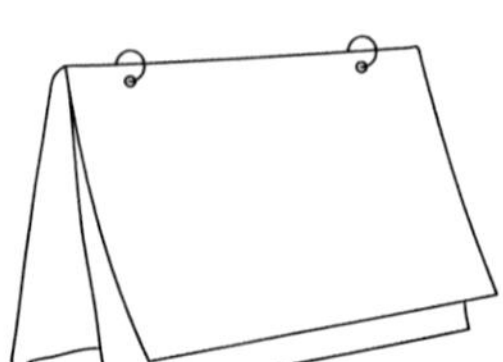

"You have become my thinking's single thought,
My heart's first love: it had no love before.
I love you as no love on earth is wrought,
I love you now and love you evermore."

"You're a fine one for tramping around,"
the bandit girl said to Kai.
"I'd like to know – do you really deserve
to have someone run to the end of
the world just for your sake?"

"Language, which he had learnt from his mother. The corn-fields and meadows were surrounded by large forests, in the midst"

*"A mermaid has not an immortal soul,
nor can she obtain one unless she wins
the love of a human being. On the power
of another hangs her eternal destiny."*

"Now, if we only had as many casks of butter as there are people here, then I would eat lots of butter!"

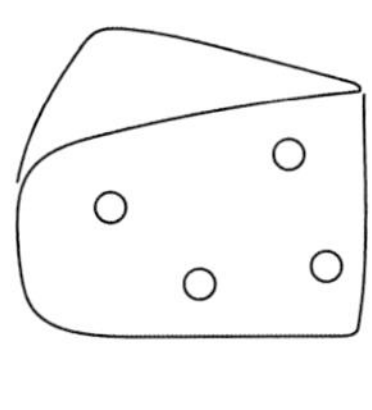

*"It was clear to me, as I glanced back over my earlier life,
that a loving Providence watched over me,
that all was directed for me by a higher power."*

*"But if the star should set,
even while I am penning these lines,
be it so; still I can say it has shone,
and I have received a rich portion."*

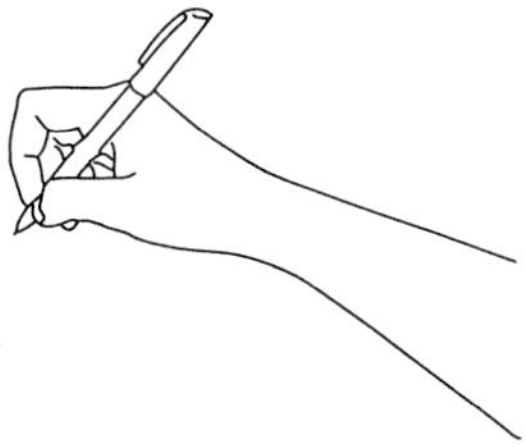

"His wedding morning would bring death to her,
and she would change into the foam of the sea"

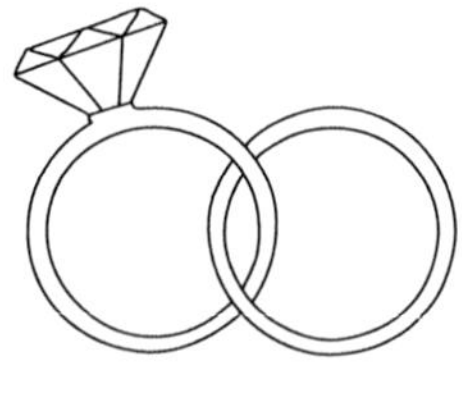

AND
ABOVE
ALL
BEWARE
OF
THE
CAT

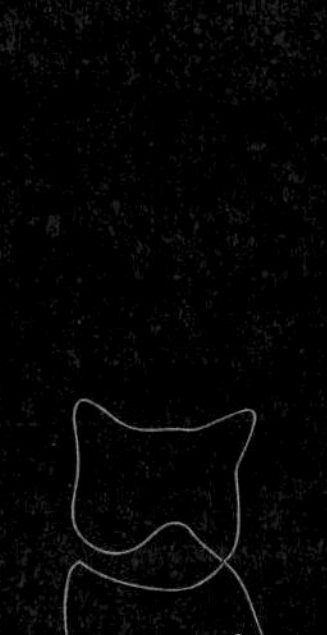

"I only do His will, replied Death.
I am his gardener.
I take all His flowers and trees,
and transplant them into the gardens of
Paradise in an unknown land.
How they flourish there,
and what that garden resembles,
I may not tell you."

"Each time I think that the song is ended...
something higher and better begins for me."

"She was so young that love was still a game to her.
She was being neither fair nor clever,
but Babette was only nineteen years old."

"And the Top spoke no more of his old love; for that dies away when the beloved objects has lain for five years in a roof gutter and got wet through; yes, one does not know her again when one meets her in the dust box."

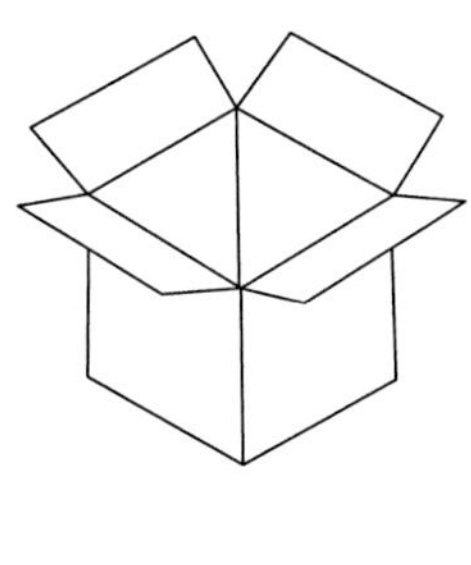

"Where are your sons?" asked the prince. "Well, it's not so easy to give an answer when you ask a stupid question!" said the woman."

"Her tender feet felt as if cut with sharp knives, but she cared not for it; a sharper pang had pierced through her heart."

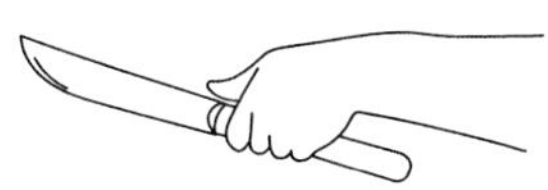

"When a storm was coming on, and they anticipated that a ship might sink, they swam before it, and sang most sweetly of the delight to be found beneath the water, begging the seafarers not to be afraid of coming down below."

"We cannot expect to be happy always...
by experiencing evil as well as
good we become wise."

"Time is so fleeting that if we do not
remember God in our youth,
age may find us incapable of thinking of him."

"No one would allow that he could not see these much-admired clothes; because, in doing so, he would have declared himself either a simpleton or unfit of his office."

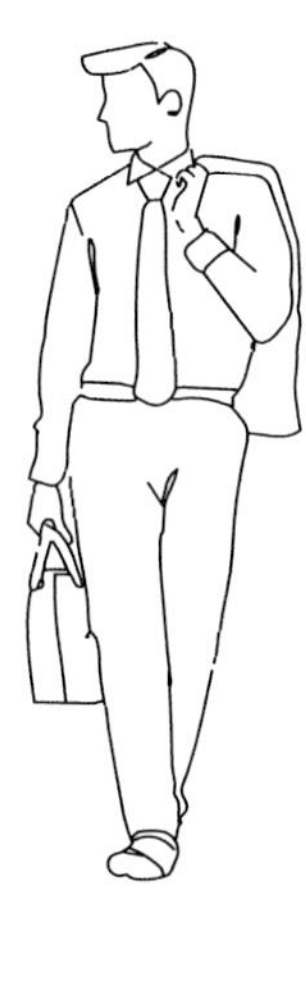

“The heart that one can see clearly,
for the most essential things are invisible”

"Most of the people who will walk after me will be children, so make the beat keep time with short steps."

"Yes, it always pays when the wife believes and admits that her husband is the wisest man in the world and that whatever he does is right."

HOW LARGE THE WORLD IS

"Now he is certainly sailing above,
he on whom my wishes hang, and in whose
hand I should like to lay my life's happiness.
I will dare everything to win him
and an immortal soul."

"Yes, it is vto be alive! Indeed,
the Bottle inwardly sang of all this, as do young poets,
who frequently also know nothing about the things of
which they sing." From The Bottle Neck"

*"And she put a wreath of white lilies
round her hair, but every petal of
the flowers was half a pearl."*

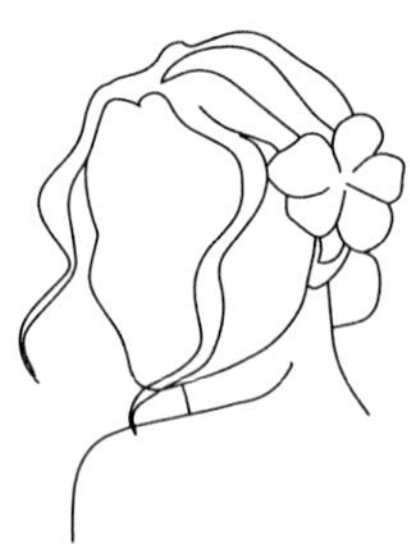

"I think I will sit on it a little while longer,"
said the duck,
"as I have sat so long already,
a few days will be nothing."
"Please yourself,"
said the old duck, and she went away."

"Cry so strange that it frightened him."

I WILL FLY TO THOSE ROYAL BIRDS

"Roses bloom and cease to be,
but we shall the Christ-child see"

"The right sort (of story) come of themselves: they tap at my forehead and say 'Here we are."

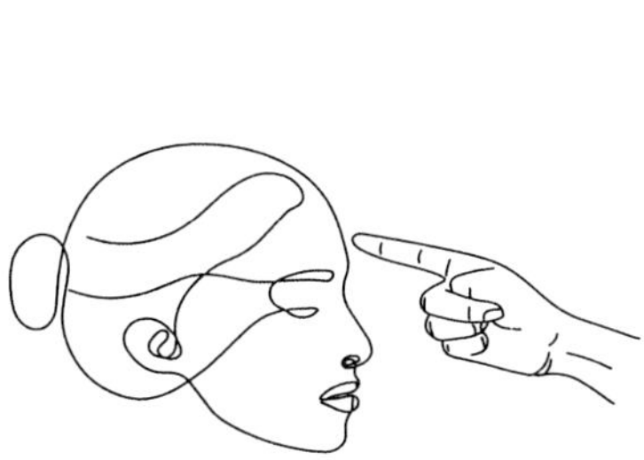

"Early in the morning, a peasant,
who was passing by, saw what had happened.
He broke the ice in pieces with his wooden shoe,
and carried the duckling home to his wife.
The warmth revived the poor"

"There was once a king's son. Nobody had so many or such beautiful books as he had. He could read about everything which had ever happened in the world, and see it all represented in the most beautiful pictures."

"Because she could not go near all these wonderful things, she longed for them all the more."

"Well, that's not easy to answer when the question is so stupidly put..."

"Grant not my prayers, when they are contrary to Thy will, which at all times vmust be the best."

"How little do the wisest among us know of that which is so important to us all."

"Superbe! Charmant! exclaimed the ladies; for they all used to chatter French, each one worse than her neighbor."

DELAYED
IS
NOT
FORGOTTEN

"No death is sweeter than this,
and no rose redder than the blood that flows."

"The most wonderful thing in the world is to make somebody happy."

"Pop, pop," sounded in the air, and the two wild geese fell dead among the rushes, and the water was tinged with blood."

"The angel plucks a large handful of flowers, and they carry it with them up to God, where the flowers bloom more brightly than they ever did on earth."

"But these are small troubles,
people will say. Yes, but they are drops
which wear hollows in the rock."

"He reached a poor little cottage that seemed ready to fall, and only remained standing because it could not decide on which side to fall first"

"There was once a bundle of matches,
and they were frightfully proud
because of their high origin.
Their family tree,
that is to say the great pine tree
of which they were each a little splinter,
had been the giant of the forest."

"Every town, like every man, has its own countenance;
they have a common likenessand yet are different;
one keeps in his mind all their peculiar touches."

"And the pea was put in the museum,
where it can still be seen,
if no one has stolen it."

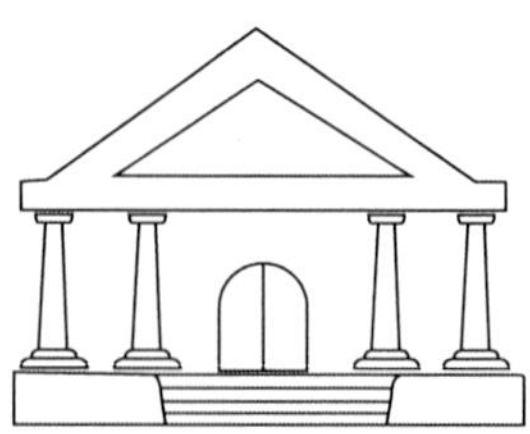

"Life is full of tough choices, indeed."

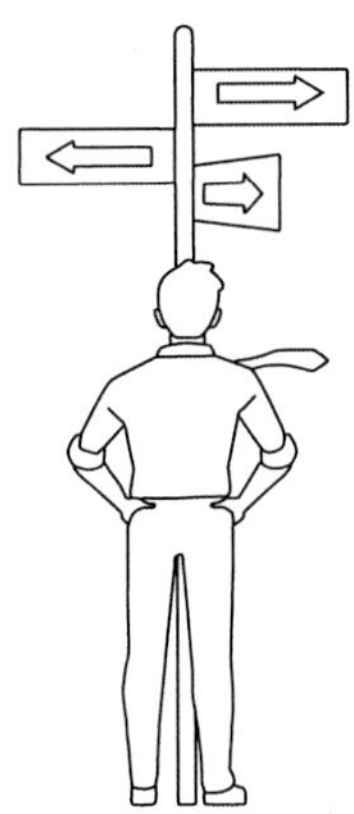

"Nothing is too high for a man to reach,
but he must climb with care and confidence."